HELPING HANDS AND SMILING FACES

Getting Cooperation On Household Chores

A Family Power Series Booklet

By
John F. Taylor, Ph.D.

Illustrated by
Gregory Griffith

Revised/Reprinted 1995
copyright © 1989
mar·co products, inc.

Published by
mar·co products, inc.
1443 Old York Road
Warminster, PA 18974

All rights reserved, including the right of
reproduction in whole or in part in any form.

ISBN: 1-884063-75-6 (Volume 2)
ISBN: 1-884063-73-X (Volume Set)

Printed in the U.S.A.

CONTENTS

INTRODUCTION **1**
   To The Reader 1
   Order Is Important 1
   Work Is Rewarding 2
   Balancing Work And Play 3
   The Habit Of Helpfulness 3
   Chores Prepare Children For Adult Responsibilities 5
   Chores Teach The Joys Of Work 5
   Children Want To Help 6
   Children Want To Belong 7
   Your Role Is Crucial 8
   Your Attitude Is Important 9
   Developing Routines And Systems 10
   Keeping Work Before Play 11

COMMON HOUSEHOLD CHORES **14**
   Bathroom Chores 14
   Bedroom Chores 14
   Mealtime Chores 15
   Pets 16
   Picking Up, Dusting, And Mopping 18
   Trash 19
   Outdoor Chores 19
   Special Occasion Chores 20
   Car And Truck Chores 20

HELPFUL TECHNIQUES **21**
   Assigning Chores 21
   Gearing Chores To The Child 22
   Using Charts 23
   Using Boxes And Other Methods 25
   Adding Interest And Variety 26

CHORE-RELATED PROBLEMS **30**
   Tying Performance To Allowance 30
   Getting The Job Done 30
   Tiring Of The Task 32
   Be Sensitive To Your Child's Needs 32

CONCLUSION **34**

INTRODUCTION

TO THE READER:

One problem common to most families is that of getting children to cooperate in performing regular household chores. Beds go unmade, rooms remain uncleaned because parents are unable to get their children to do chores that have been assigned and are willing to do the chores for them. Or, in another common scene, parents hesitate to assign chores because the children can't or won't do a good job and the parents end up doing all the household chores themselves!

Yet we all know of families where everyone pitches in to help and the chores get done regularly and without undue hassle. What makes the difference? Perhaps it is basically a difference of attitude.

ORDER IS IMPORTANT

A house of order is a house of love. Children as well as adults appreciate order. Uncleanness and disorder get in the way of happiness. Neither you nor your child can enjoy your home unless it is reasonably clean and routines are orderly.

Order exists in two ways:

1. In structure, which means placement of objects, things are in their place, clean, and usable.
2. In process, which means actions of people, the family's routines and activities result in an orderly home.

When their is order in both structure and in process, your child feels more secure because life is more dependable and the events are more predictable.

Order saves energy. Looking at or staying in a chaotic, disorganized situation drains energy and makes people feel tired. When there is not enough order within a person's home, a great deal of energy is wasted dealing with the disorder. People who end up with large amounts of effective, productive energy usually have orderly places in which to live and work.

WORK IS REWARDING

When adults have poor attitudes toward work, they often pass those negative ideas on to children. For example, adults sometimes act as if work were something terrible, something to be avoided. Such persons split all activity into two types: (1) having fun and enjoying themselves, or (2) working and not enjoying themselves. In this framework, work becomes bad and play becomes good. The person wishes away the work day, looking forward to the time after work. During the work week, such a person talks only about the joys of the weekend.

On the other hand, good attitudes toward work can also be shown to children. Work can have its own built-in rewards. A productive share-in-the-work attitude can lead to personal happiness and to success in life. Work does not have to be unpleasant. It does not have to make the worker feel like a slave. Such attitudes can make a difference in the home where everyone—adults and children—can contribute to the order and pleasantness of the entire household. Through work in the home, your children can experience a sense of strength and mastery.

BALANCING WORK AND PLAY

Just as the adult world does not consist of constant heavy responsibility, a child's world should not be one of constant play. In order to gain more enjoyment from play, your child needs to experience work. The experience of work helps to develop good traits that will last a lifetime.

THE HABIT OF HELPFULNESS

People are rarely happy if they are completely idle. Satisfaction comes from being independent, from accomplishing tasks, from mastering skills, from meeting challenges, from learning new things, and—most importantly—from making a contribution to others. You can use common household chores to help your child learn these important lessons of life. By participating in household routines, your child will learn self-discipline, promptness, neatness, appreciation of quality, and the importance of helping others.

An additional advantage of training your children in the habit of helpfulness is that they can manage better in crisis situations. If there is an illness or an emergency, a child who has learned various homemaking responsibilities will be able to take over key functions for the family.

Encourage the helping habit early in your child's life, so that it becomes a natural part of living. To a little child there is no difference between doing a chore and playing. The very young child thinks that doing chores amounts to play, and that chores are more fun if done along with the parent. Encourage your young child to accept responsibilities by standing next to you at the kitchen sink, rinsing spoons, putting them into the dishwasher, towel drying pots or mixing bowls, or by sitting beside you at the workbench and handing you work.

Everyone needs to feel important. Avoid turndowns because they become turnoffs. Phrases like "you're too little," "Hurry, Sally can do this faster than you" can do great harm to your small child's desire to help.

You will find it much easier to train a child in the helpfulness habit early rather than to try to undo different patterns when the child gets older. It is easy to train a very young child to put away one toy before getting out another one. When your child is little, you'll need to give more step-by-step instructions. Aid and inspect your child's efforts to guide efficient performance.

Provide your young child with the opportunity to do something parallel to what you are doing. Have the child use a child-size broom, a small dust cloth, or a toy lawn mower and "work" beside you. Even if the child's activity is not efficient, you are teaching a lesson that is far more important. Slowly build choice into the situation, so that your child gains an increasing ability to control and influence the types of chores that are done.

CHORES PREPARE CHILDREN FOR ADULT RESPONSIBILITIES

Teach your child to enjoy work. Work is a way to learn skills and prepare for adult life. Introduce chores as opportunities to learn how to be a good mother, father, house guest, homemaker, and a generally happier person. Motivation will be greater for accomplishing chores if your child understands that helping keep an orderly living area will be an important part of adult life.

There is a danger in being too role-bound to gender stereotypes in exposing your child to household chores. It is freeing to your child to know how to take care of various aspects of your household. Well-rounded childhood experiences with various types of household chores helps prevent awkward dilemmas in adult life. Many men, for example, in college, the military, or traveling as part of their business, profit greatly from knowing how to care for their clothing and how to cook. Likewise, women need mechanical skills at home, in work settings, and in respect to automobiles.

CHORES TEACH THE JOYS OF WORK

There are several sources of personal satisfaction from sharing in household chores. If you help your child experience these feelings, you will be leading your child into a pattern of helpfulness that will bring a lifetime of happiness.

Your child will enjoy doing chores more when their direct personal benefit is made clear. The preparation for adult living that has already been mentioned is a good example. Point out that your child's skill is growing and that the increased skill will be of direct benefit to your child now and in the future.

One of the most powerful motivators is the awareness that others are directly benefited by your child's actions. Help your child understand how chores improve the well-being of the family members. This process of making your child aware of the social impact of chores can be done privately with a direct statement by you, or it can be done during a family discussion.

Instead of competing with and defeating other people, train your child to compete with the challenges in the environment by overcoming obstacles and accomplishing tasks. Most things can be made to be more beautiful, made better, controlled for a good purpose, or otherwise handled in a productive way. To turn a few scrap pieces of wood into a bird feeder, to mend a broken item, to rake leaves, to mow a lawn, to trim a hedge, or to remove clutter from a room are ways of gaining mastery over objects and causing them to be moved or modified in a helpful way. The child who is able to make things better by handling objects is realizing material impact and will feel stronger, more competent, and more capable than the child who is deprived of such opportunities.

Clear, direct expressions of appreciation and thanks for the child's contribution go a long way toward training in the habit of helpfulness. Don't make the mistake of taking chore accomplishments for granted. Gratitude statements are easy to combine with social impact and material impact statements, so there is no reason to omit them when talking with your child about chores.

Comment on the large amount of effort and devotion shown by your child in a way that shows that you recognize and understand the child's feelings. Nobody likes to try hard at a task and have others dismiss the effort by not noticing it.

CHILDREN WANT TO HELP

Your child's natural tendency is a desire to help and to participate. Deviation from this natural tendency is the result of some unusual stress or force. Draw on this natural tendency as much as you can rather than relying too much on artificial incentives.

As a toddler, your child often asks to help. Encourage your child's attempts to explore the environment and to experience social and material impact. The small child who wants to handle toys and throw them around, for example, can be encouraged to stir things in mixing bowls as a way of helping you prepare meals. This kind of rechanneling nurtures your child's basic desires to help and starts the process of training for a lifetime of helpfulness.

There may be many opportunities for your child to be the one in charge, so that you are helping your child, rather than your child's always having to be your helper. Preparing a meal, washing dishes, searching for items on a shopping list, or doing laundry are opportunities for your child to enjoy a new level of helpfulness by working together with you.

CHILDREN WANT TO BELONG

Instead of teaching that chores are your responsibility and that you are dumping your responsibilities onto your child, teach that chores are a shared part of family living. Your child needs to learn that home is *our* home, that family is *our* family, and that chores are *our* chores. Your child is not doing mother's chores for mother or father's chores for father; instead, the family's chores are being done by all members of the family for the family.

Explaining family routines encourages cooperation and gives a sense of family unity. Denied these opportunities, your child's thoughts will turn selfishly away from the family's needs, and your child may become reluctant and uncooperative. When the entire family pitches in, your child will associate work with pleasure. Expect contribution and diligence rather than doubting that it will occur. If you need to give a specific instruction, avoid statements like *"I* need you to do...."; instead try to put the emphasis on the overall need of the family by statements such as *"We* need you to..." or *"The family* needs this done..."

Teach your child that work is not for "somebody else," but is for all family members. The doing of dishes presents an excellent opportunity to teach this lesson. The person doing the dishes did not eat off of all the dishes, nor eat with all of the utensils, nor drink from all of the cups. Don't let your child avoid chores with an excuse such as "I didn't do it, so I shouldn't have to clean it up."

YOUR ROLE IS CRUCIAL

Some amount of side-by-side activity is called for while you maintain a leadership role. Doing all the work at home is not your responsibility. However, seeing that it ultimately gets done and that your child develops the habit of helpfulness *is* your responsibility. Organizing and supervising chores are also your responsibility, and every family member should participate in keeping household order. Your functions are to instruct in how to do chores correctly and to maintain a list of all tasks that have to be done. Be instructive, supervise, organize, and participate by helping your child do chores and by doing some of the chores yourself. Your participation should not be done merely as proof of your helpfulness in the home. Avoid both extremes:

1. Leading but never participating, and
2. Participating too much.

YOUR ATTITUDE IS IMPORTANT

You should set an example of being a good hard worker. Put as much joy, enthusiasm, and vigor into your chores as you can, without being phony. Think of chores as an opportunity to present before your child some things that you can do to train for successful living. The best attitude is one of training your child in the habit of helpfulness, both by instruction and by your example.

It may be helpful to teach your child some of the activities that you do during the day. If indicated, try offering to switch roles with your child for a day, and have your child do all that you do. In this way, your child will gain a deeper appreciation for the effort that you regularly devote toward the family.

Get in the habit of doing things *with* your child rather than just *for* your child. Neither of you is working *for* the other. If you mop, have your child clean the baseboards. When you vacuum, have your child dust. When you mow the lawn, have your child help sweep the walk. Your child will then have a feeling of companionship *with* you and of accomplishing something *with* you. You can also avoid the dangerous role of chasing after your child while you are apparently trying to get out of work.

Don't be bullied into taking too much of the chores on your own shoulders or allowing your child to avoid responsibility and participation. If you take on all responsibilities, your child will feel free to do whatever brings pleasure at the moment rather than doing what is important.

There are many ways in which a cooperative arrangement can occur in the doing of chores. Train your child early, for example, to help bring groceries in. When the groceries arrive, everyone is to pitch in; even the smallest child can carry small items. Everyone gains a sense of responsibility. It is a fun adventure to see how quickly all food can be put away. The group goal adds interest; if all food is put away before the timer goes off, for example, the family will have a treat.

Be willing to look at the humorous side of household chores, the condition of the family, the decor of the child's room (Early Tornado), the hectic morning, and the other aspects of home organization that need constant attention. Household responsibilities are difficult enough without overly stern and pessimistic attitudes on the part of the parent. Try to have an *in spite of* attitude, rather than a *because of* attitude about the effects of household stresses on your actions and mood. Be determined to have a smooth morning *in spite of* chore responsibilities, rather than grumbling *because of* those responsibilities. Your attitude really does make a difference.

DEVELOPING ROUTINES AND SYSTEMS

The unexpected task is what your child is most likely to rebel against. If household chores are natural and expected parts of daily routine, your child is more likely to cooperate happily. Chores should be done at regular times of the day. Don't expect your child to wait for last minute instructions from you. Just as it is important for you to divide your day into various time segments, it is also important that your child do the same. Knowing that the day is divided adds a dimension of safety and order that is reassuring to your child. A dependable time for play and a predictable time for work are important. Enforce deadlines and periods during which family routines start and stop.

You will want to develop a system for distributing jobs among family members for a specific period of time. You'll want to decide on how to supervise and how to check on chore completion. And you might want to consider some type of motivation or incentive.

The goal of the system is to get the home and everything in it orderly by having everything clean, usable, and in its place, with everyone involved in accomplishing this order. No system always works perfectly. Be willing to change various aspects of your system occasionally.

Supervise closely at first. Teach your child how to do the job well, with clear and specific guidelines. If necessary, take your child step-by-step through the task until the desired performance occurs.

When establishing rules and guidelines, use aspects that are countable and specific. Give finishing touch information as needed to your child, and a chance at that one specific chore later on.

KEEPING WORK BEFORE PLAY

The key principle is that work comes first before play. Your child will both work better and play better if you lived by this guide.

Work will go better because:

- The child is eager to get the work accomplished in order to be able to start playing.
- The child realizes that delaying the work will mean less time left in which to play.
- The child is fresh and has high energy for tackling the work, because there is no vigorous play prior to doing the work.
- The child realizes that if the work is not done well enough, it will have to be done over and will interfere with play.

Play will go better because:

- The child will believe that the play has been earned by the work which has been done.
- The child knows that he/she does not have to face working after the play, so play can involve a full release of energy.
- The child does not have to be curbing the enjoyment of the play, because there is no unpleasant task to face at the end of play.

Without the principle of work before play, your child might extend playing time and then try to use the excuse that there is not enough time or energy left for getting the chores done.

In organizing your family by the principle of work before play, you are teaching additional important lessons. Children need to experience playing together with parents to gain a balanced view of the family-wide nature of work and play. Work is the highest priority. Play is an important activity that counterbalances work. Happy people are almost always hard-working people who are productive and who use play as a counterbalance to work. The goal is to work hard and play hard. Too little of either makes any person's life out of balance.

You may need to give a gentle reminder between the end of one activity and the start of another. You do not like to stop in the middle of something pleasant to do something less pleasant, and neither does your child. Don't jerk your child away from a play activity to do a chore. Give a few minutes notice, with a time to start chores and a time to stop doing them. Any failure by your child to complete the chores on time should result in the child's doing the chores at the next available moment at the expense of the child's play periods.

Each time of day has its strengths and limitations for doing chores. Popular times of day are:

- In the morning, either before or after breakfast.
- Right after school.
- Just prior to the evening meal.
- Prior to bedtime.

Take carefully into account your family's unique situation in planning your system. Most people function better at certain times of the day. If mornings are already hectic, adding chores to the morning routines may not be practical. If your child would feel overburdened by having to do chores immediately upon arriving home from school, it might be better to allow a play period after school prior to doing household chores. If the home is too messy after children have left for school, it may be best to arrange early morning chores and earlier times of arising.

COMMON HOUSEHOLD CHORES

Every family will need to develop its own list of chores. These suggestions come from homemakers who have developed efficient systems of getting household chores done.

BATHROOM CHORES

Bathroom chores can be handled smoothly by requiring each person to clean up messes as they happen. Clothes are to be put into a correct container in or near the bathroom. Used towels and washcloths are to be rehung if this is your family's routine, or are to be placed in a correct container immediately. The tub is rinsed out as the water drains out. Bath rub ring can be reduced by bubble bath. The floor is wiped with the used towel. Spilled toothpaste is immediately wiped up. Hair and mouth care items are placed on shelves or hangers. Very few items are left on counters.

BEDROOM CHORES

Most children can strip and change a bed by age seven. Be willing to go through the process with your child several times. Do not remake a bed after your child has done it. Instead, advise about or assist with remaking it. A bedwetting child should have the responsibility of stripping and changing the bed each morning, and of depositing the soiled linen in a correct container or the washing machine.

A *daily* routine for your child's room can include these types of activities: make the bed, hang up clothes, put soiled clothes in a correct container, put shoes away, clear dresser or shelf, straighten study area, close all drawers and doors, pick up anything on the floor, and empty waste baskets.

A *periodic* schedule would includes: changing bed linens; straightening the closet and dresser drawers; cleaning mirror and windows; dusting around windows, ceilings and baseboards; and vacuuming.

MEALTIME CHORES

Have everything at hand that your child may need, including a chair or stool for reaching the counter and sink. A very small child should not be expected to handle very many dishes at once or very fragile items. Place the correct number of items in the center of the table for the very small child to place when setting the table.

Mealtime chores can be shared among family members. A typical plan would involve these types of chore assignments:

Meal Helper:
Assists in preparing meal.
Helps to determine menu for that day.

Server:
Pours beverages.
Dishes food onto plates as needed.
Butters rolls or bread.
Obtains additional items from cupboard, stove, or refrigerator during the meal.
Assists in serving younger children.

Table and Chair Helper:
Makes sure table and chairs are clean.
Sets chairs in proper locations.

Sets the table, including spices and condiments.
Provides serving bowls and spoons on the table.
Clears the table after the meal.
Washes and dries the table after clearing it.
Washes and dries any spilled food on the chairs.

Floor Helper:
Moves all chairs away from the table after the meal.
Sweeps the entire eating area.
Replaces chairs.
Sweeps kitchen areas that were used in meal preparation.

Dishes Helper:
Empties dish rack or dishwasher of previous load of clean dishes.
Washes the dishes, or rinses them for loading into the dishwasher.
Loads the dishwasher.
Washes utensils and pans.
Dries all dishes, utensils, and pans as needed.
Puts dishes, utensils, and pans away.

Counter Helper:
Cleans off all kitchen counters.
Cleans stove top.
Returns ingredients used in meal preparation to cupboards.
Cleans countertop and appliances used in meal preparation.

PETS

Pets represent an important investment of money, time, emotion, service, and space. What starts out little and cute can end up big and not so cute! If the pet is a dog or larger animal, the total involvement can be similar to having another child, and

the cost of feeding the pet can exceed the cost of feeding a small child. An untrained dog may not be enjoyable because it jumps on children, chews things, barks, and may become too hard to manage or control. Other emotional considerations include pet care when the family is away, issues like how much money to spend to cure a disease or to save the pet's life, and bereavement upon the death of the pet.

Spending on pet needs can teach your child money management skills. A survey of pet owners revealed that an aquarium with fish, a hamster, a bird or a pair of gerbils represents about one-half the annual expense of a rabbit or cat and about one-fourth the annual expense of a dog. Financial investment in a pet can include food, veterinary costs, licensing, grooming, housing, discarding of animal waste, equipment for transporting the pet, cages, leashes, harnesses, bedding, filtration equipment, and temperature control devices. Financial planning can include consideration of these types of expenses, in addition to setting aside funds for the purchase of additional pets and equipment and preparing for unexpected expenses.

All should share in the responsibilities as well as the joys in owning a family pet, if the pet is indeed the *family's* pet. Incorporate pet care as a part of regular household duties. If the pet "belongs" to one or two children in the family, the ordinary responsibilities of day-to-day pet care should be theirs. Some parents purchase a pet *for* a child when in reality their choice fills their own needs rather than the child's needs. Avoid the common error of expecting too much from a child who is too young to handle these responsibilities.

Be prepared to find another home for the pet if your child won't assume a reasonable part in pet care routines. You will be correctly giving your child the logical consequence of negligence. Reassure that there can always be a next time and that your child is currently not ready for this kind of pet. Discuss the matter again a few months later.

PICKING UP, DUSTING, AND MOPPING

What is gotten out must be put back. If playmates are involved, they should also pick up their playthings, so that the burden is not entirely on your child. Have shelves, bins, or boxes available for easy toy storage.

The box system is a popular method of assisting a child with the picking-up chore. Items that are not picked up are put into a central location such as a box or hamper. There are many possible variations to this system, and you should gear it to the needs of your family. You will need to decide on these variables:

- Length of time during which the items are stored, ranging from one day to one week.
- What items are to be put into the box.
- Who will be allowed to put things into the box (usually everyone in the family).
- The process by which items can be obtained from the box (by request, doing a chore, paying a small fine, etc.)

The box system should be done in a pleasant, lighthearted way as a decision of the entire family. To add interest in the method, give the box a name.

The box becomes a temporary container for household clutter. It can be decorated. Unclaimed items may be auctioned off if the person does not wish them anymore or does not want to pay the fine for them. Items not claimed can be given to charity. Any fines collected can be used for a family fun project.

Be careful with polish or cleaner in spray cans. Instruct your child to spray the cloth, rather than spraying the furniture.

Make sure that your child is strong enough to handle a mop and bucket efficiently. A very young child will need special help if asked to do this chore. Teach your child the principle of not mopping so that the child is trapped in a corner. Also instruct the child to avoid walking on the wet part until it is dry. Skating over the wet floor with old towels is a fun way to dry the floor.

TRASH

Take your child through the garbage or trash procedure the first time step-by-step. Assess your child's ability to:

- Carry the small trash container or plastic liner bag outside to the garbage can.
- Lift the lid off the garbage can.
- Lift the small trash container over the lip of the garbage can and turn it upside down into the garbage can.
- Fasten the lid after filling the garbage can.

A hose should be available for rinsing the small container after each load is dumped and for periodic rinsing of the garbage can.

OUTDOOR CHORES

Many families have a variety of outdoor chores that need to be done regularly or from time to time. Yards and gardens need watering, weeding, mowing, harvesting, raking, feeding, and sweeping. Seasonally, you may need to trim shrubs, put away lawn furniture, put up or take down storm windows, or shovel snow. Keeping garages and other work areas in good order provides opportunity for even the smallest child to be of help.

SPECIAL OCCASION CHORES

In addition to regular chores, there are always special events that bring extra work for the whole family. Birthdays and religious occasions have their own traditions. Children will find new meaning in the events if they are involved in preparing for them.

In addition to such formal special occasions, the family vacation, trips to visit relatives, and even family picnics can provide times for building the helpfulness habit.

CAR AND TRUCK CHORES

Car and truck care can provide opportunities for working with your child or for your child to earn extra money. Routine needs include checking fluids, washing the outside, washing the tires and chrome, vacuuming the inside, and washing the windows and mirrors.

HELPFUL TECHNIQUES

A family meeting is an arena in which your child can learn why your family needs its routines. You can discuss the need for chores as well as the various methods of getting them done.

Concerns about specific chores should be discussed by the whole family. You will want to discuss the natural consequences of having a chore remain unfinished during this meeting. Rules and guidelines are best given in the family meeting. Expectations for the quality of job performance, in general terms, are given there. How-to's for each chore can also be given and demonstrated.

When teaching about a chore, offer help at the beginning, or toward the end of the child's attempt. Don't do the whole chore for your child, and don't have your child standby merely to watch you do the chore. Have your help available but withheld; don't hover over your child.

Show the entire family how to repair and maintain items used in chores. Instruct in how to change sweeper belts, how to oil tools and appliances, how to change light bulbs, and similar aspects of maintaining household equipment.

ASSIGNING CHORES

If you have never assigned chore duties before, explain what system you will use. Your child must understand that you are not suddenly making many new demands. Present a list of proposed job assignments, but try to allow the child some choices from the list. Deprived of such a voice and choice, your child may not want to cooperate.

The length of the list of chores and the criteria for a job well done will vary with the age and skill level of each child. Decide how often the chores are to be done and when during the day or week they should be done. Explain what the duties are in each task, welcoming suggestions to make the chore easier or more helpful to the family. Be sure to explain why the chores are needed; your child needs a chance to do things for a reason other than that you said so. Try to solve any problem situations as they arise. It is often best to have the whole family in on the discussion.

GEARING CHORES TO THE CHILD

Suit the chore to the age and readiness of your child. Simplify the chore if necessary, but leave enough challenge so that your child can grow by doing the chore and can have a genuine sense of accomplishment. Offer increasingly more challenging chores after easier ones are mastered.

An older child will feel resentful and overworked if a younger child is excused from chores just because the older child can do them more quickly or thoroughly. If chores are rotated, be sure to include the youngest child capable of performing each chore into the schedule. Also be willing to perform yourself any chores your child is completely unable to perform.

A chore rotation system allows assignments to be distributed fairly. No one receives easy tasks while others receive more difficult or less enjoyable ones for a long period of time. Try to give your child a voice in deciding which chores are to be done, when, and by whom. Chores can be rotated at various intervals—daily, weekly, bi-weekly, monthly, or quarterly.

The routine isn't routine if the system is changed too often. Also, too frequently changing the system prevents you from keeping track of whose turn it is to do which chores, and your child might become confused about the assignments. The "It's not my turn" complaint can be the result.

Assigning chores each day by telling each child what to do each day puts unnecessary stress on you and makes your child too dependent. Instead, chore assignments are more easily handled by a rotation procedure that uses a nonverbal method.

USING CHARTS

Job charts simplify things by adding order and eliminating the need for verbal instructions to your child. In designing the best chart for your family, you will need to decide:

- Tasks to be listed.
- Name or description for each task.
- Method of marking when task is completed.
- Standards for monitoring chore performance by whom and how frequently.
- Points or rewards (if used as part of your system).

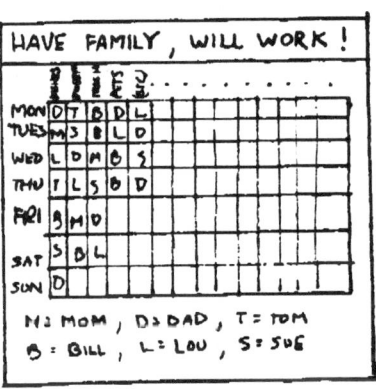

A good chart can train your child in the habit of helpfulness and be a welcome change from nagging. The chart will inform the entire family of who is supposed to do what, when, and over what period of time. It will also indicate who has accomplished the tasks. It should serve as a reminder of what the chore assignments are.

Simple variations will allow a chart to last for a long time. For example, a permanent list of jobs can remain on the chart, while the names of the persons doing the jobs can vary from time to time.

It is also possible to design a chart so that a new sheet of paper can be taped over the grid with new data on it. A chart listing the persons' names and the days of the week might have a separate index listing of all the chores, for example, from 1 to 25. The grid would contain numbers 1 through 25. Each person would look into the square for the day of the week to discover the chores assigned for that day. When rotation occurs, a new sheet of paper would replace the grid, having a different assignment of the code numbers on it.

Charts can be designed which also allow one to mark accomplishment. Checking off chores as they are completed allows your child to see an indication of the amount of work done and gives "credit" for the work. Various methods of marking for accomplishment are available. Use a method that appeals to your child.

Personal goals can be included in the chart along with chore assignments. Personal goals have to do with your child's improvements in various areas. They include such topics as educational achievement, cleanliness, helpfulness to siblings, or politeness to parents. Your child's accomplishment of personal goals can be recorded along with accomplishment of chores.

An ordinary calendar is a simple and effective variation. Your child can initial the calendar placed next to the chore assignment list as each chore is completed. Initials in the square indicate that your child has completed all chores for that day.

A floor plan chart is another common version of charting. The floor plan can be painted on a large piece of wood or stiff cardboard. Chore assignments can be written on tags hung on hooks for each room on the chart. Rotate simply by moving the tags onto different hooks.

Charts can be made attractive in many ways. They should be geared to the child. Include a clever title and appealing colors, and place it at your child's eye level.

Several methods are available for helping a preschool child use job charts. Help your child cut out pictures of chores from magazines and paste them onto cards or construction paper. If magazine pictures can not be found for each chore on your chart, draw some with crayons.

Color coding can assist a small child in reading a job chart. A red card in the child's grid space, for example, may mean to sweep the floor. Your child can help color the item or paste a picture on it.

Another method is to take pictures of your child doing the chores. Paste the photos onto sturdy cards as chore indicators. Pictures of a completed chore, such as a clean room or a table set with each dish in place, can also be used.

USING BOXES AND OTHER METHODS

A card file box may be more useful in some families than a wall chart. Have a separate card for each task. Your child rotates the card to the back of the file after the chore is done.

A magnetic bulletin board is another option. Brightly colored contact paper can turn a metal cookie sheet into such a board. Clever kitchen magnets can hold the chore assignment information.

The pocket or envelope method has many variations and will fulfill a wide variety of family situations. Large open manila envelopes can be glued to posterboard, with two pockets for each child. One pocket is for chores to be done, and the other is for chores that have been completed. Small cards with chore assignments written on them can be placed in the "to be done" envelope each morning.

Simple pockets can be made by stapling a horizontal strip of cardboard with your child's name on it to a wood or heavy cardboard backing. Staples are placed every few inches, so that pockets are formed along the strip of cardboard. Chore assignment cards can be placed in each pocket or moved to the next pocket when the chores are done. This system makes rotation especially easy by allowing all chore assignment cards to be moved to the next child's pocket.

The names of chores can be written on small key tags or on 3" x 5" cards with holes punched in them. The cards or tags can be hung on hooks screwed into a board. Your child can move the card or tag from one hook to another after the chore is done. If the chart is given only to remind of assignments, there may be no need to move the cards or tags except when chores are to be rotated.

ADDING INTEREST AND VARIETY

You can add interest and variety by having for a time, perhaps summer, a completely random method of chore assignment, so that there is no need for rotating assignments. There are several options available.

Try drawing papers or cards with chore assignments on them from a container passed from one person to another until all assignments have been taken. When all chores have been completed, the papers or cards are returned to the container and used again for next day's or week's chore selection.

Or you could allow your child to choose from a list of chores. This method is less strict because not all of the chores will be done at any specific time.

Spinner methods allow many variations in random chore assignment. Use a colorful homemade spinner to point to the person or chore, with each person having the opportunity to spin the spinner to decide which chores will be done and by whom.

Whether your family is using assigned chores or randomly chosen ones, there are many ways to make the performing of household chores more fun for all. Try using some of these techniques:

Surprise Cards:
Put additional cards into the job assignment file box or additional tags onto the job chart board. The additional cards indicate surprises and special privileges to delight your child. They are discovered after the chores are done, as cards or tags are being shifted to the next location or are being rotated by your child. Try placing the surprise card last in a series of cards, so that it is discovered after all chores have been done.

House Fairy:
The House Fairy can be a make-believe person who, like the Tooth Fairy, visits and leaves surprises. The House Fairy can leave such items as notes, cards announcing favors and privileges, pennies, or even pieces of candy. This method provides a light-hearted approach to inspecting your child's work. The House Fairy can make a visit about once a month or once a quarter, when extra thorough cleaning has been required.

Choo-Choo Train System:
Everyone enters a room together, and each person cleans part of the room. The whole room is improved in just a few minutes. The train then goes to the next room. At the end of the train's trip through the house, the family stops at the "depot" for refreshments.

Family Work Time:
One of the most common methods is to have a special time that is set aside for all family members to do chores and routines. The set time can be daily, weekly, or both. The goal is to get everyone involved. When the entire family pitches in, your child will learn to associate work with the pleasure of family unity. Your child will experience a sharing of burden and will develop increased closeness to the family. A brief cleanup period before bedtime, during which the entire family pitches in, allows all family members to awake the next morning to a clean and organized house.

Planted Surprises:
Placing surprises around the chore area helps your child learn to clean furniture, rooms, and cars thoroughly. Your child would clean the items anyway and is not cleaning just because of the planted surprises. They become an adventure that adds to the total experience. Simply tell your child to keep any money discovered while cleaning.

Courtesy Cards:
Small cards the size of ordinary business cards, 1" x 3", with the words, "Courtesy of _____" can be signed by your child and placed in the rooms in which major tasks have been completed. All will then know which jobs have been done and by whom. Your child will have given a personal signature to the effort and therefore will have greater pride in doing a good job.

Chore Games:
A simple game is to time chores as the family does them together. For example, see how much time it takes for the family to clean up a certain room. A record can be kept of the times for various rooms. The family can earn a treat by cleaning a room faster than before.

To train a young child in helpfulness, have your child write on walls with a damp sponge or cloth. This is an interesting example of mixing work and play. You can use a plastic dropcloth, so that your child can use a small container of water. Because most dirt is in the lower half of the wall, you will have less wall washing to do. Having seen the wall clean and having worked toward the goal of washing it, your child will be less eager to dirty walls in the future.

Damp mopping the floor is another fun chore for your child, during which letters or numbers can be written with the mop on the floor.

While picking up toys and clutter, your child can throw some of the items into a wastebasket or toy box from a distance, rather than carrying them over.

Faces can be drawn on old socks, and your child can play puppet games while dusting.

Spend a few moments to create more ways to make a game out of a chore!

Chore Parties:
Your family can have a party with refreshments after the weekly family cleaning period. A fun outing after your family's work period can also help make chores less of a burden. Singing or listening to music while working together as a family can help chores go smoothly.

CHORE-RELATED PROBLEMS

No matter how carefully you outline chores to be done, you will from time to time run into problems. Think through in advance how you will handle the most likely ones.

TYING PERFORMANCE TO ALLOWANCE

A common error is to tie allowances too closely to chores, so that your child loses the sense of what the allowance is for. An allowance is not a reward for doing chores. There does not have to be a strong connection between allowances and the performing of routine household responsibilities.

One answer is the base and supplement method. A certain base amount is given, to be supplemented with an amount that reflects how well your child has performed household chores and routines. Another approach is to have required chores as well as optional chores. Your child must do the required chores first. Call these "no pay" chores. After your child is done, he/she is free to earn various amounts of money by choosing from among several "for pay" chores.

GETTING THE JOB DONE

The amount of checking that you do on your children is an important issue. One of the most frequent errors is living by the motto: "always check to see that every job is done well." Such airtight supervision is possibly needed in a military situation where issues like tact and trust are not involved. Your family, however, is not the Army or the Marines. Love and trust can not grow when the monitoring method is too strict. This attitude implies distrust, puts too much responsibility on you, and can cause your child to feel unappreciated. You are also putting yourself in the role of an adversary, more of an enemy than a friend.

Instead, teach your child how to do the chore. Then trust that it is done if your child says it is, unless your child's behavior patterns in the past lead you to a different conclusion. Conduct an *occasional* check if needed, and note any problems. At a calm moment, bring any concerns to your child's attention or discuss them the next time your family gets together. Always consider changing routines, rather than simply stating that your child is not trying hard enough.

If you never check the chore performance, your failure to do so may imply a careless "I don't care" attitude on your part. Checking should be done often enough to show that you are concerned, but not so often that it implies distrust of your child.

Be wary of taking on too much responsibility. Do not try to decide on all the chore assignments, give the list to your child each day, remind your child to do the chores, and insist on some kind of artificial incentive. To do all of these activities is too much involvement and would create a top-heavy system that gets very little accomplished in terms of training your child in an attitude of helpfulness.

Do not do for your child what your child is capable of doing. By the process of learning-by-doing, your child will learn to take on increasing responsibility. Encouraging your child to be responsible for as much of the chore procedure as possible will bring satisfaction and a sense of personal strength.

If you find that a job must be redone or touched up in some way, be tactful and kind in your comment. Speak to your child in a helpful manner and suggest ways in which the routine can be improved so that this type of error does not occur again. Beware of redoing a job for your child, because to do so implies that your child's work and contributions count for nothing. Don't offer help unless it is requested or its need is painfully obvious.

TIRING OF THE TASK

What will you do when your child tires of the assigned task? Your responsibility as a parent is to teach your child that if obligations are not met, the consequences will be unpleasant for all concerned. These consequences will deprive your child of a sense of belonging and of the good will of others.

Your best attitude is one of giving choices. Your child either does the task and receives the benefits from doing it, or your child fails to do the task and receives the previously set up consequences of that failure to perform. Stay as outwardly uninvolved as possible, and avoid nagging and reminding your child about the task. If you use too much verbal pressure, your child will automatically balk and will not have a sense of owning personal responsibility for getting the chore done. The issue for your child will then become a struggle with you over your right to order that your child do the chores. Times when the whole family is together are logical times to handle this kind of issue. [1]

BE SENSITIVE TO YOUR CHILD'S NEEDS

When your child grumbles about having to do a chore you might at first be tempted to say "Don't gripe!" or "Do as you are told!" However, such a reaction is your own version of grumbling and puts you on a child's level. It also causes you to miss a golden opportunity to respond to some important needs that your child has.

---

[1] For a through discussion of logical consequences, see *Creative Answers To Misbehavior*, available from **MAR•CO PRODUCTS, INC.**

It is wiser to show empathy for your child's concerns. State that you understand your child's misgiving and that there are unpleasant aspects to the chore. After sufficient empathy has been given, provide encouragements.

Grumbling means that your child's needs are not being met and that perhaps the system needs to be addressed, either individually with your child or in the family meeting. Take your child aside and discuss in detail the nature of your child's concerns. Though grumbling looks and sounds like misbehavior, it typically carries with it genuine concerns that should be addressed in a loving and helpful way. If grumbling persists, change the system in ways that lower the stresses on your child.

"I'll do it later" might mean that your child is trying to avoid an unpleasant job also. Empathy and a searching inquiry should be involved when exploring how the system could be revised to meet your child's needs better.

The most frequent errors that parents make in supervising their children are to nag and remind. Repeated problems in your child to follow through on a chore indicates one or more of the following:

- The proper attitude of helpfulness has not yet been reached.
- The chore must be broken down into smaller units.
- Some adjustment must be made in chore assignments.

Daily bickering, reminding, and coaxing by the parents are not part of an effective system. They are an indication that the system needs to be changed.

CONCLUSION

Common household chores can be used to help children develop the habit of helpfulness. Homes in which routines and systems are clear and in which each member of the family participates to the limits of his or her ability are loving and happy homes. By having a positive attitude you, as a parent, can help your child prepare for adult responsibilities and learn that work as well as play can be fun.

You will need to survey and list your family's needed routines. By talking and working together, you can develop a system that works. The result will be a well-ordered home in which household chores are performed promptly and with increasing efficiency with *HELPING HANDS AND SMILING FACES!*

ABOUT THE AUTHOR

John F. Taylor, Ph.D. is a family psychologist in private practice in Salem, Oregon. He is the author of such well-respected books as *Helping Your Hyperactive/Attention Deficit Child; Person To Person: Awareness Techniques;* and *Diagnostic Interviewing Of The Misbehaving Child.* He has published numerous articles in newspapers and journals. He is president of *Sun America Seminars* and frequently gives presentations to professionals throughout the United States and Canada on topics pertaining to strengthening the family.

The father of eight children, this respected psychologist and author brings his personal and professional experience together in this exclusive booklet series.

Resources by John F. Taylor, Ph.D.
available from
mar∗co products inc.

COUNSELOR SURVIVAL SERIES BOOKS:
Anger Control Training for Children and Teens
Diagnostic Interviewing of the Misbehaving Child
Motivating the Uncooperative Student
Positive Prescriptions for Negative Parenting
The Attention Deficit/Hyperactive Student at School
Understanding Misbehavior

FAMILY POWER SERIES BOOKLETS:
Correcting Without Criticizing
Creative Answers to Misbehavior
Encouraging the Discouraged Child
Helping Hands and Smiling Faces
Listening for Feelings
No More Sibling Rivalry!

AS WELL AS:
Answers to A.D.D.—The School Success Kit (Videotape)
Helping Your Hyperactive/Attention Deficit Child
Person to Person

TO ORDER CALL: 1 • 800 • 448 • 2197